MENTORING YOURSELF

THE BECOMING OF SOMEONE WHO BUILDS

AYUSH GARG

Copyright © Ayush Garg
All Rights Reserved.

This book has been self-published with all reasonable efforts taken to make the material error-free by the author. No part of this book shall be used, reproduced in any manner whatsoever without written permission from the author, except in the case of brief quotations embodied in critical articles and reviews.

The Author of this book is solely responsible and liable for its content including but not limited to the views, representations, descriptions, statements, information, opinions and references ["Content"]. The Content of this book shall not constitute or be construed or deemed to reflect the opinion or expression of the Publisher or Editor. Neither the Publisher nor Editor endorse or approve the Content of this book or guarantee the reliability, accuracy or completeness of the Content published herein and do not make any representations or warranties of any kind, express or implied, including but not limited to the implied warranties of merchantability, fitness for a particular purpose. The Publisher and Editor shall not be liable whatsoever for any errors, omissions, whether such errors or omissions result from negligence, accident, or any other cause or claims for loss or damages of any kind, including without limitation, indirect or consequential loss or damage arising out of use, inability to use, or about the reliability, accuracy or sufficiency of the information contained in this book.

Made with ♥ on the Notion Press Platform
www.notionpress.com

For the ones who stayed when I had nothing to offer.
For the sleepless nights that became turning points.

And for the builder in me, who refused to give up — even when the world
gave no reason to continue.

Contents

Contents

FOREWORD

*This isn't a book filled with answers.
It's filled with attempts.*

*Every chapter comes from lived experiences — not from
podiums, but from the ground, the cracks, the quiet.*

*I never planned to write this book. But somewhere between
falling apart and figuring it out, I ended up living it.*

*And maybe, just maybe, a part of this story will remind you
of your own.*

Preface

I didn't plan to write a book. I just needed to make sense of things. Thoughts, emotions, frustrations, breakdowns, tiny wins, people I trusted, people who disappeared, plans that failed, and those rare days when everything clicked. I was tired of carrying it all in my head, so I started writing—one entry at a time.

Not for Instagram. Not for some future TED Talk.

Just... for me.—not to teach, not to impress, but to stay sane. Somewhere along the way, I realized these weren't just random notes. They were patterns. Lessons. Truths I hadn't said out loud. They reminded me of who I was becoming, even when I didn't feel like I was moving at all. These words became stories. Stories became lessons. And here we are.

This isn't a how-to guide. It's not a motivational manual either. It's just a window. Into a mind that never stops building. Into the loop of burnout and hope. Into the raw, beautiful mess of becoming someone you can be proud of—even when the world isn't clapping.

If you find yourself here, maybe you're also figuring things out. Still rebuilding. Still learning. Still showing up.

So here's my journal. Read it like a conversation, not a lecture. You're not alone in the in-between.

Acknowledgements

To every person who walked with me—whether for a moment or a mile—thank you.
To the ones who left—you taught me what not to carry forward.
To my family, for grounding me. To my cats, for reminding me to rest.
To my community—especially those shaping Kumohana—thank you for giving my work a reason to evolve.
To AI tools and systems that let me work smarter and lighter—you are the teammates I never expected to have.
To every version of me that kept showing up, even when the world didn't applaud—this is for you.
This book is proof that nothing we go through is wasted.
Even the pauses. Even the pivots. Even the parts that didn't make sense at the time.
To every reader holding this book:
Thank you for showing up.
Thank you for staying curious.
Thank you for mentoring yourself.

Prologue

We don't become who we are all at once.
We get there through late nights, uncomfortable choices, messy attempts,
and uncelebrated consistency.
This isn't a success story.
This is a survival story.
Of someone who had no roadmap, no backup plan, and no perfect pitch.
Just a need to build — something, anything — that made sense in a world
that didn't.
And while I was busy building things...
I realised, I was building myself all along.

I

The Journal I Never Thought I'd Write

I never planned to write this book.

Not because I didn't have things to say—but because for the longest time, I didn't think they mattered.

I was the kind of person who journaled quietly. Not the poetic, calligraphy-pen kind of journaling. The messy kind. The unfiltered thoughts typed on my phone's notepad at 2:43 a.m. The scattered sentences on the back of old bills. The scribbles in diaries I never intended to finish. There was no structure, no "morning pages," no journaling routine. Just a need to make sense of what was happening inside me—because I didn't know how to say it out loud.

Somewhere in those scribbles, this book began.

Not as a project.

As survival.

I didn't start writing because I had answers. I started because I had too many questions.

Too many phases where I felt stuck between who I was and who I was trying to become.

Too many days that looked productive from the outside—but were filled with doubt, distraction, and quietly asking myself,

"Is this really it?"

People think building a business—or even just a life you're proud of—starts with vision. Strategy. A goal.

For me, it started with confusion.

And silence.

I remember one afternoon where I had absolutely nothing lined up—no client calls, no work, no emails. Just an eerie stillness. I should've used the time to rest, or ideate, or 'build something.' Instead, I sat on the floor of my room, just staring at the wall, wondering if this is what people meant by freedom. If this is what "being your own boss" really felt like—quiet, uncertain, and not at all how I imagined.

That day, I didn't journal anything profound. I wrote three words:

"What's the point?"

No hashtags. No motivation. Just that.

But here's the thing about writing—even on your worst day, it listens.

And over time, those random entries, those half-finished reflections, became patterns.

They showed me things I had ignored about myself for years.

Like how I chased validation more than I chased clarity.

Like how I kept switching projects, not because they failed—but because I never believed I deserved to win with any of them.

Like how I could coach others to grow, but struggled to take my own advice when no one was watching.

So I kept writing.

Not for likes. Not for a book.

But to keep myself company on days I couldn't recognize the person I was becoming.

And one day—unexpectedly—it hit me.

"What if this mess... is the method?"

What if the rawness, the failures, the slow rebuilds, the side detours—what if that is the real mentorship people need?

Not a perfect guide.

Not a "7 steps to success" template.

But a voice.

A reflection.

A brutally honest, compassionate voice that says—

"Yes, it's confusing. Yes, you'll question everything. Yes, sometimes even breathing feels like effort. But no, you're not lost. You're just building."

And that's when I knew.

This isn't a manual.

It's not even a memoir.

It's a witness.

Of becoming.

Of failing.

Of trying again.

Of building quietly while the world watches louder people.

This is not the kind of book I ever thought I'd write.

But maybe that's the whole point.

You're not reading a polished version of me.

You're reading a mirror. A rough draft. A notebook of someone who is still learning to trust his own journey.

So if you've ever sat in your own silence, doubting your direction...

If you've ever felt like you're building something no one understands...

If you're still trying to figure it all out...

Welcome.

This Journal is for you.

II
The Business You Build When You're Broke

It didn't start with a pitch deck.

Or a domain name.

Or some genius idea scribbled on a napkin.

It started with an old camera lying idle in a corner of my house—dust-covered, half-forgotten—like the life it once captured was now long gone.

It belonged to my father. He had run a studio for years. Photo shoots, wedding edits, local events—the kind of hustle you don't see celebrated on LinkedIn. He had moved on from it, grown tired, maybe a little burned out. And the gear, once treated like gold, now sat untouched.

But I hadn't outgrown that fire.

I was still in college. CS was on one side. BBA was wrapping up. The future was uncertain. But there was one thing I knew—I didn't want to wait. I wanted to earn. I was tired of asking for pocket money. Tired of feeling dependent. Tired of wondering when things would begin.

So I picked up that camera and told myself,

"Let's just start."

No brand name, no business plan. Just hunger.

Later, I called it Working Wolves. At the time, it was just... me.

I began offering free shoots—weddings, portfolios, events, anything. I wasn't confident, but I was willing. I didn't know much, but I showed up. I remember traveling with friends, shooting content with the energy of Bunny from Yeh Jawaani Hai Deewani, thinking maybe, just maybe, this would go somewhere.

But here's the hard part no one talks about.

Nobody pays the beginner.

No one trusted me enough to give me a proper gig.

No one believed this was more than a hobby.

I was that "guy with a camera"—not a creator, not a professional.

And still, I kept showing up.

Not because I was fearless—but because I was broke.

And the silence that came from having no real income?

It echoed loud.

I watched people around me get campus placements.

Friends discussing salaries, offer letters, LinkedIn profiles.

Me? I was pitching free shoots and editing on an outdated laptop at 2 a.m.

Eventually, the pressure got to me.

I had a degree. I could speak well. I knew how to present myself.

So I applied at a call center.

No shame. Just survival.

I needed money—not to shop or show off—but to breathe without guilt.

To take my own decisions without asking for ₹500 every time I wanted to eat outside.

So I took the job. Picked up shifts. Answered calls. And on the side, I still carried my camera like a secret life I hadn't let go of.

I used to feel bad about that.

Like I had failed.

Like I had sold out.

But now I realize:

That was me learning to build without applause.

That was me choosing to stand on my own—even if it wasn't Instagram-worthy.

There's a different kind of business that gets built when you're broke.

It's not the kind with seed funding and startup culture.

It's the kind where your rent is your reason.

Where your first ₹2,000 matters more than someone else's big fat invoice.

It's the kind of business that doesn't need validation to be real.

It's real because you're in it—every day, every shift, every try.

If you're there right now—broke, confused, figuring it out in silence—let me tell you something people don't say enough:

You're already building.

You're building grit.

You're building awareness.

You're building trust in yourself—even if the market hasn't caught up yet.

You don't need a co-founder.

You don't need a vision board.

You just need a reason. And if that reason is survival, it's good enough for now.

The business I built when I was broke taught me more about myself than any course ever could.

And that's something I'll never trade.

III

Not the Golden Boy, Still Chose Gold

I wasn't the kid who topped exams.

I wasn't on stage with medals around my neck.

My name wasn't the one parents used to scold their kids into studying harder.

I was the "good enough" student.

The one who passed, sometimes failed, but always showed up.

The one who didn't cause trouble, but also didn't shine.

And for a while, I thought that meant I wouldn't matter much.

In my town, success was a straight line: get into science, aim for IIT, land a government job or become an engineer. The rest? Side characters in someone else's story.

So when my cousin—my mentor, my guide—moved away for his own career, I was left navigating it all alone. I followed the advice I was given: "Take science. It's safer."

But safety, it turns out, isn't always smart.

I wasn't failing because I was dumb.

I was failing because I was disconnected.

From myself. From what made me curious. From what made me me.

The subjects didn't make sense. The pressure blurred my thinking. I started questioning my own potential. And eventually, I cracked. I had to switch. From science to commerce. From clarity to chaos.

That switch came with whispers.

"He couldn't handle it."

"He didn't try hard enough."

"He's just average."

Maybe they were right.

But what they missed was this: I kept going.

I picked up Company Secretary as a new direction.

Cleared the foundation exam. Failed the next.

Started again.

I wasn't racking up achievements.

I was racking up resilience.

Somewhere in the middle of all this, I was also helping at home.

Borrowing tools from my father's old studio.

Creating side projects. Learning through trial and error.

Designing. Shooting. Writing. Editing.

Not because someone told me to.

Because I wanted to.

And in those quiet hours—when I was figuring things out alone—I found gold.

Not the kind that comes in certificates or trophies.

The kind that gets built in silence. In seasons of doubt. In rooms where no one claps.

I wasn't the golden boy.

But I chose gold anyway.

Not the gold of public praise, but the gold of private growth.

The kind of gold that doesn't rust with time.

The kind that shows up in how you respond to failure, not how you pose with success.

If you've ever felt like you missed your "golden child" phase...

If your story didn't start with top marks and glowing reviews...

If you had to fight your way through average labels and background noise...

You're not late.

You're not less.

You're just choosing a different kind of gold.

The kind that doesn't fade.

Because it was never polished to impress—

It was built to last.

IV
Fail Fast, But Don't Forget the Bruises

They say fail fast.

They don't mention how it feels when you actually do.

No one talks about how it messes with your confidence, how it feels like your chest tightens a little every time someone asks,

"So, how's work going?"

You smile. You nod. You give the safe answer.

Because no one wants to hear that you're not getting paid, that you're tired of asking for favours, that your inbox is a ghost town and your ideas feel stale before you even try them.

But that was my reality for a while.

I had picked up the camera, dusted off my father's old equipment, and named my effort Working Wolves. It felt cool. Raw. Unpolished in the best way. I didn't know how to run a business, but I knew how to show up.

So I did. Over and over again.

Free shoots. Random edits. Late-night calls. Travel gigs with friends. Chasing stories. Creating content.

Hoping, wishing, praying that one of these projects would finally bring in some money.

But no one paid.

They loved the enthusiasm, sure.

They admired the hustle.

But to them, I was still a guy "trying something."

And that "trying" phase felt like a lifetime.

I started wondering if this was worth it.

If maybe I had hyped up my own dream too much.

If maybe I wasn't cut out for this.

If maybe, just maybe, I should give up.

And then I did something I didn't expect: I applied for a job at a call center.

It wasn't my dream job. It wasn't even a good job.

But it gave me something I hadn't had in months—a sense of control.

I needed money—not validation, not attention, not likes. Just money.

So I took the job. Logged in. Took calls. Learned the script. Hit the metrics.

And went home with a paycheck.

It felt weird.

On one hand, I was relieved.

On the other, I felt like I had betrayed my creative self.

But here's what I didn't realize back then:

That choice didn't kill the dream.

It funded it.

That job taught me discipline.

It reminded me that consistency mattered more than charisma.

It gave me a routine, a rhythm, a reason to keep showing up.

And most of all, it taught me this:

Failing fast isn't the lesson.

Failing consciously is.

Anyone can burn through an idea and call it growth.

But if you're not learning from it, not reflecting, not asking yourself the real questions—what's the point?

I failed fast.

But I also got bruised.

And those bruises taught me more than any course ever could.

So don't glorify the fall unless you're willing to talk about the wounds.

Let them teach you.

Let them hurt for a bit.

And then—let them heal into something solid.

Because what you build after the bruise...

That's where your real story begins.

V

The Start Nobody Applauded

How was your childhood?

Not the version you rehearse for relatives or interviews.
The honest one. The one that shaped you quietly—without permission, without a plan.

Mine was loud, curious, and a little chaotic.
I didn't grow up around motivational books or mentors with frameworks.
I grew up around DSLR cameras, Casio keyboards, cracked CPUs, and Adobe Photoshop tutorials being taught in the other room.

My father ran a studio.
He trained his staff on how to edit wedding videos and design album layouts.
While other kids were memorizing multiplication tables, I was learning how to adjust white balance and reformat memory cards.

We had more keyboards than textbooks at home.
More wires than toys.
And if anything broke, we fixed it—not because we were tech geeks, but because we had no choice.

Phones? I opened them all—Nokia, Motorola, even Virgin Mobile—just to see what lived inside them.

Music? I taught myself how to play the Casio.
Sometimes I played drum pads. Sometimes harmoniums.
Never professionally. Always playfully.

I didn't know it then, but something was growing in me:

The urge to figure things out without needing permission.

By the time I was in 9th grade—around 2007—I had already built my first website.

It was called SpyCamIndia.

My dad had brought back spy cameras from Chandni Chowk, and I thought I could help him sell them online.

I used WordPress, created basic listings, took product photos, and even learned how to post backlinks in random tech forums—without having a clue what SEO meant.

No orders came in.

No money. No real traffic.

Just effort.

And when I showed it to a few people, they said,

"Nice. But why are you wasting time on this?"

So I stopped.

Not because I failed—but because no one clapped.

And when no one claps, you start to believe maybe you're just making noise.

Then life moved forward.

My cousin—the one person who believed in my madness—left for his studies.

Suddenly, I didn't have that guiding voice anymore.

I moved cities. Changed schools.

Got introduced to a new world where people asked things like,

"What's your stream?"

"Which coaching are you joining?"

"Science or commerce?"

I chose science.

Because it sounded safe. Smart. Respected.

But nothing in me aligned with it.

Not the syllabus. Not the people. Not even the teachers.

The boy who once built websites at 13 was now drowning in chemistry formulas he didn't believe in.

That quiet confidence from childhood? It started slipping.

And I didn't even notice until it was gone.

Sometimes I look back and think:

"What if someone had just said: 'That's cool.'
What if someone had seen that website and said: 'You're onto something.'
Would that have changed things?"

Maybe.

But what matters more is that even without applause, I kept building.
Quietly. Silently. Without a label or outcome.
Because it felt like me.

That's what no one tells you:
You don't need validation to begin.
You just need curiosity.
And the courage to follow it—even when no one is watching.

So if your start feels unfinished...
If your early work never got noticed...
If you've been building in the background...

It still counts.

Because the start that nobody applauded...
might just be the reason you don't give up when things get real.

VI

When Survival Becomes the Strategy

Have you ever had a season where your only goal was to just keep going?
Not to thrive. Not to achieve. Just... make it to the next month without falling apart?

That's what this chapter of my life looked like.

After switching streams, after stepping off the path everyone else was racing through, I was now walking in slow motion.
No spotlight. No clarity. Just trying to hold it together.

I got into a nearby college—not because it was great, but because it didn't ask too many questions.
The campus felt like a compromise. The atmosphere was loud, unfocused, and wildly different from the environment I had grown up in.
No one was dreaming. Everyone was just passing time.
And maybe, so was I.

But something inside me didn't shut off.
There was a pulse. A pull. A quiet whisper that said, "This can't be it."

I started taking trips to Delhi in between classes.
No real plan—just curiosity.
I visited old areas. Walked into bookstores. Attended workshops.
And looked for places where people seemed to have some idea of what they were building.

That's when I found the Company Secretary course.

It sounded sharp. Professional. Structured.

Something that could give me direction. Something I could say "I'm working on."

So I joined weekend classes.

It wasn't passion—it was survival.

But sometimes, survival is what carries you long enough to find purpose again.

I juggled college on weekdays and CS on weekends.

There were moments I felt hopeful again—like maybe I was piecing something together.

I passed the foundation exam in my first attempt.

But the next level came with two separate groups of exams.

Harder. Heavier. Time-hungry.

I couldn't keep up.

I failed both.

Not because I didn't try—

but because I was trying to do everything with a battery that was already dying.

By now, I was stuck in a loop:

Too tired to start again, too scared to stop completely.

So I did what many of us do when dreams start slipping through our fingers—

I looked for a job.

Something. Anything.

Just to feel useful again.

What this phase taught me:

Sometimes, you don't grow through passion.

You grow through pressure.

You don't always have the luxury to dream big.

Sometimes, your only job is to stay in motion.

And if you're in that phase right now—don't shame yourself for surviving.

There is wisdom being formed in you.

Patience. Grit. Endurance.

The kind that doesn't come from success stories.

The kind that only comes from staying in the story.

VII

The Job You Take to Prove You're Not Failing

Have you ever taken a job just so you didn't have to say you had nothing going on?

Not because it excited you. Not because it matched your skills.

But because it gave you a salary—and a little silence from the questions people kept asking?

That's what the call center was for me.

After the CS results came in—and I failed both groups—I didn't know how to explain myself anymore.

I was studying. Then I wasn't.

I was building something. Then I wasn't.

I needed a win, any win—even if it didn't feel like one.

So I got the job.

The headset. The fixed shift. The elevator that always smelled of stress.

It didn't matter what I was doing.

What mattered was that I was doing something.

The first few days felt like oxygen.

I had somewhere to go. I had a routine. I had a payslip.

But very quickly, I realized something deeper:

I was shrinking.

I was answering scripts on repeat. Solving problems I didn't care about.

Coming home tired—not from effort, but from emptiness.

I wasn't building anything.
I was just pressing pause on the noise in my head.
And there's a kind of quiet that looks like stability on the outside...
but eats you alive from within.
I lasted four months.
Four months of early logins, timed breaks, polite voice tones, and a growing fear:
"What if I get stuck here?"
I looked around at people who had been doing it for years.
Nice folks. Good people.
But you could see it in their eyes—many of them had stopped dreaming.
And I couldn't afford that.
Not because I was better.
But because deep down, I knew something:
If I don't leave now, I'll learn how to stay.
And that scared me more than failure ever did.
So I quit.
I didn't have a backup plan.
But I had one thing that most jobs can't give you:
myself—free again.
What this taught me:
Sometimes, we accept things just to feel like we're not falling behind.
But keeping pace with the wrong life is worse than pausing for the right one.
If you're in a job that's slowly dulling your instincts...
If you've stopped creating, exploring, asking...
Give yourself permission to leave—even if it makes no sense to anyone else.
You don't owe the world explanations.
But you owe yourself the chance to still believe.

VIII

When Plans Don't Pay, But Something in You Still Stays Alive

Ever had a phase where nothing worked, but something in you just wouldn't let go?
Where every "logical" thing said you should move on,
but a quiet voice kept saying, "Not yet."

That was me—right after I left the call center.

No job. No exams. No plan.
Just this weird, stubborn energy that I couldn't kill.

I told myself I'd study again.
This time, I'd go all in for government exams.
I got the books. Made a timetable. Even stuck to it for weeks.

And for a while, it felt right.

Then came the news:
The exam date got postponed. By three months.

Something broke.

It wasn't just about the delay.
It was the realization that I was constantly chasing timelines that weren't mine.
Always reacting. Never creating.

And that realization hurts deeper than failure.
Because failure at least feels final.

This?

This was limbo.

One afternoon, when the silence got too loud, a friend called.

He had a small product business. Needed help listing items.

Writing descriptions. Setting up some backend things.

"Just for a while," he said.

Nothing fancy.

I said yes.

And here's where it gets interesting.

The moment I started working on those listings—

Something shifted.

It felt familiar.

Too familiar.

Like *déjà vu.*

I was back to uploading products. Adjusting images. Writing titles.

Just like I had done on that Wordpress website I made back in 7th grade.

Except now, I wasn't a kid playing with pixels.

I was someone who had lived through failure, doubt, burnout—and was finally putting old skills to work with new perspective.

And for the first time in years,

I didn't feel behind.

I felt home.

It wasn't a job.

It was a loop closing.

What I had once done for fun,

was now doing for survival—

and slowly, for strategy.

What this taught me:

Not everything you tried early in life was a waste.

Some things just needed to be paused until you were ready to use them well.

Sometimes, you have to fall far enough to recognize what you were holding all along.

If you're lost right now,

look backward—not to repeat your past,

but to reclaim the tools you've been ignoring.

They're still there.

Waiting for you to remember.

IX

The First Time It Feels Like Freedom (Even If There's No Money Yet)

You know that feeling when things start to make sense—not because the world changed, but because you finally caught up with your own potential?

That's what this chapter was for me.

I was still broke.

Still figuring things out.

Still eating basic meals and stretching phone data plans like a full-time sport.

But something was different now.

I wasn't scared.

I had something better than stability—

I had momentum.

During that time, I was constantly scrolling through Amazon Seller Central, Snapdeal dashboards, Wordpress plug-ins.

I didn't fully know what I was doing—

but I knew more than I gave myself credit for.

And that curiosity?

It led me somewhere unexpected.

I started wondering:

What do these digital marketing coaching centers really teach?

I mean, I had already been doing the work. Running campaigns. Listing products. Troubleshooting plugins.

So I borrowed money.

Actually—a friend lent it to me.

He offered to pay half the fee as barter for some help I'd given earlier.

I used it to enroll in one of the top-rated institutes for digital marketing at the time.

And here's what shocked me:

Almost everything they taught, I already knew.

In fact, in most classes—I was ahead.

While they explained theory,

I had stories.

While they showed screenshots,

I had dashboards.

While others struggled to understand how a campaign works,

I had already run three—with learnings, insights, and mistakes under my belt.

It was the first time in years I felt genuinely confident.

Not because someone praised me.

But because I realized:

I didn't wait to be taught.

I had taught myself.

That experience gave me something money couldn't buy:

Proof.

Proof that I wasn't just trying random things.

I was building something that others were just beginning to understand.

And the best part?

I still wanted to learn more.

Not from textbooks, but from testing, trying, tweaking.

What this taught me:

Don't wait to be qualified to begin.

Start doing, and the world will catch up later.

Sometimes, when you walk into a room expecting to learn—

you realize you've already been living the lesson.

And that moment?

That's the start of real freedom.

Not financial freedom.

But the kind where you finally believe that you know what you're doing.

Even if the world hasn't noticed yet.

X

Why Motivation Didn't Work on Me

I've read enough quotes to know what motivation sounds like.
I've watched enough reels to know what it's supposed to look like.
But the truth?

Motivation didn't save me.

Motivation didn't show up the day my account hit zero.
It didn't sit beside me when I was questioning everything at 1:37 a.m., staring at a half-finished deck, trying to convince myself it was still worth it.

Motivation didn't get me out of bed.
Fear did.
Guilt did.
Sometimes, just the need to not feel useless for another day did.

I've seen so many people talk about "how to stay motivated."
The planners, the quotes, the reels with piano music in the background—
as if a good soundtrack can pull you out of creative quicksand.

But for me?

Motivation has never been the fuel. It's been the fluke.

It shows up when it wants.
It disappears without warning.
It's like trying to build a business on candlelight—pretty for a moment, but it flickers and dies when the room gets cold.

What I needed wasn't motivation.
What I needed was a system to hold me when I couldn't hold myself.

There was a phase when I had no clients, no clarity, and no clue what day of the week it was. I'd stay up late pretending to work—switching tabs, watching tutorials, rewriting captions, refreshing Gmail—and still go to bed with nothing to show for it.

I kept thinking: maybe tomorrow I'll feel fired up.

Maybe a new reel will spark something.

Maybe I just need a better playlist, a cleaner desk, a new idea.

But day after day passed, and motivation never showed up on time.

So I did something I hadn't done before.

I stopped waiting for it.

I created rituals instead.

Small. Repeatable. Grounding.

I made my bed—even if I had nowhere to go.

I opened my notebook—even if I didn't know what to write.

I showed up at my desk—even if all I could do was move one tiny task forward.

Not to feel productive.

To feel stable.

Because motivation comes and goes.

But momentum is built through rhythm.

And rhythm is what saved me.

People think burnout comes from doing too much.

Sometimes, it comes from doing too little of what keeps you centered.

I wasn't tired because I worked hard.

I was tired because I kept waiting to feel inspired before I acted.

And that's where most of us get stuck.

We think we need to feel good to do good work.

We think we need to be in the "right zone" before we write, or plan, or pitch.

But the truth?

Sometimes your best work comes on the worst days.

Not because you felt it—but because you refused to disappear.

One night, while journaling—half-awake, half-broken—I wrote this line without thinking:

"Discipline is the love language you offer to the future version of you who still believes."

And I kept writing it until I started believing it.

Because showing up—even when it feels useless—is an act of hope.

It's how I reminded myself that I don't just want success.
I want self-respect.
I want to look back and say, "I didn't bail on me."
So if you're stuck, tired, uninspired, or doubting your worth because you don't feel motivated—
Don't wait.
Don't scroll.
Don't overthink.
Just pick one tiny thing.
Make your bed. Drink the water. Write the email. Open the blank doc.
Not to impress anyone.
Not to go viral.
Not even to finish.
Just to say,
"I'm still here."
And sometimes, that's all it takes to begin again.

XI

Every Skill I Thought I Had... Wasn't Enough

There was a time when I thought I had it figured out.

I had the language.

I had the tools.

I knew how to open Canva, edit reels, pitch ideas, run ads, write copy that sounded sharp.

I could sell myself in an elevator.

I could answer questions in meetings with calm confidence.

I could handle deadlines, design decks, and deliver strategies like I was born for it.

And for a while, it worked.

Clients nodded.

Colleagues respected me.

Friends asked for advice.

But then something happened that shook me:

A project I believed in completely—

One I had built from scratch, poured my energy into, lost sleep over—

Failed.

And not softly.

The client pulled out.

The feedback stung.

The effort went unnoticed.

It wasn't just a lost deal. It was a lost mirror.

Because up until then, I thought I was "skilled."

And now, I wasn't so sure.

That night, I wrote in my journal:

"What if I've just been good at looking busy?

What if I've confused momentum with mastery?"

That question stayed with me for months.

I started revisiting everything I thought I was good at.

Design? It was okay—but I lacked depth.

Writing? Sharp, but inconsistent.

Strategy? Decent—but only when I felt confident.

Teamwork? Functional—but not leadership-ready.

Self-management? Nonexistent on bad days.

What I had were starter skills.

Enough to begin. Not enough to build something sustainable.

And that broke me in the best possible way.

Because it humbled me.

It made me sit down, slow down, and rebuild from scratch.

I stopped looking for shiny new tools and started fixing the shaky foundation.

I re-learned how to communicate.

Not just to impress, but to connect.

I rewired how I handled pressure.

Not by reacting, but by regulating.

I studied real branding—not just colors and fonts—but human psychology, business patterns, emotional storytelling.

I realized being "skilled" wasn't the end goal.

Being useful, self-aware, and adaptive—that's what mattered.

You see, it's easy to collect skills today.

YouTube, courses, reels, AI—you can mimic brilliance.

But real work? It's not about imitation.

It's about depth.

And depth comes when you stop decorating your ability and start digging into your discipline.

Here's what I learned the hard way:

A confident tone doesn't equal a confident self.

A portfolio doesn't always reflect your patience.

Being good at something today doesn't mean you'll stay good at it tomorrow.

If you don't sharpen it, it blunts.

If you don't stretch it, it shrinks.

If you don't check your ego, it leads you into rooms you're not ready to stay in.

So I stopped saying, "I'm good at this."

And started saying, "I'm working on it."

It's a simple change.

But it saved me from staying stuck in a version of myself that was once enough—but no longer is.

And if you've ever felt like you were good at something... but the world still said "no"?

It doesn't mean you're not good.

It means you're being invited to grow deeper.

Don't run from that.

Because what comes after that moment of collapse?

That's where the real skill begins.

XII
The Silence That Built My Confidence

Confidence, I used to think, looked like volume.
Like the loudest person in the room.
The one who walked in with answers, gave speeches, held eye contact, and never second-guessed themselves.

And I tried to become that person.
I tried to speak louder, dress sharper, act like I knew what I was doing—even when I didn't.

But no matter how many calls I crushed or meetings I faked my way through...
I'd come home and still feel like I was borrowing someone else's skin.

Then, life did something strange.
It took away the noise.
No meetings.
No notifications.
No validation.
Just space.

Uncomfortable, echoing space.

I had finished a few projects, paused client work, and decided to take a break—but the break became a void. People moved on. The phone stayed silent. The inbox slowed down. And I found myself sitting alone with my own voice.

At first, it terrified me.

I remember one night, lying on my mattress, staring at the ceiling fan spinning like a thought I couldn't slow down. The silence wasn't peaceful—it was personal. It made me confront questions I had been avoiding for years:

"Who are you when you're not building something?"
"Can you still trust yourself when no one is clapping?"
"Do you like yourself when the world isn't watching?"

I didn't have answers.
But I started writing again. Not content. Not captions. Just... thoughts.

One line. Then two.
Then paragraphs that turned into late-night journal sessions.
No goal. No plan. Just expression.

And slowly, the silence became a mirror.
It showed me how much of my identity was built around being seen.
How my confidence was stitched together from other people's praise.
How I equated performance with purpose.
And how deeply I needed to be liked to feel valid.

But in silence, I wasn't being liked. I was being real.
There were no filters.
No "How's business going?"
No one to impress.

Just me—and the slow, painful, but grounding process of rebuilding my confidence from within.

Confidence, I realized, isn't about proving you're good enough.
It's about knowing you'll be okay even when you're not at your best.

It's not about being perfect.
It's about showing up anyway.

Some of my most confident moments didn't come on stages or in wins.
They came:

When I admitted I didn't have the answer.
When I took rest without guilt.
When I said no to work that didn't align.
When I chose honesty over image.
And the reason I could do that?
Because silence taught me how to listen to myself again.

So if you're in a phase right now where things are slow, quiet, disconnected...

Lean in.

It might feel like nothing's happening.
But everything is.
You're learning to hold space for yourself.
To not depend on applause.
To not chase noise just to avoid your own thoughts.
That kind of inner confidence?
It's quiet.
But it's unshakable.
It doesn't scream.
It doesn't sell itself.
It simply is.
And once you find it...
You won't trade it for anything loud again.

XIII

When You Start Building Without Realizing You've Already Begun

Have you ever looked back and realized... "Wait, I've already started"?
You didn't plan it. You didn't announce it.
But one task turned into ten, and suddenly, you're not stuck anymore—you're moving.

That's exactly what happened to me.

I didn't sit down with a business plan.

I didn't write a vision board or declare a 5-year roadmap.

I was just helping a friend with his product listings.

Fixing titles. Polishing descriptions. Arranging banners. Creating little systems to make things smoother.

But something started growing—in me.

My energy shifted.

I started waking up with direction again.

And I wasn't working for money. I wasn't even working for recognition.

I was working because it felt natural.

Like this was exactly what I was meant to do all along.

I didn't know it then, but that project...
was the seed.

From that tiny corner of content and listings,
I started exploring how digital platforms really worked.

Funnels. Creatives. Campaigns. UX writing. Branding.
I wasn't "studying" them.
I was living them.

I was learning faster than any course could teach me—because now, I had skin in the game.

And slowly, I started taking on more.

More projects.
More ownership.
More me in the process.

What started as a "favor" became a full-time habit.

And without realizing it,
I had transitioned from someone looking for work
to someone building their own ecosystem.

No office.
No team.
No title.

Just a curious kid—now older, sharper, and finally in his zone.
What this taught me:
Not all building looks like building.
Sometimes it looks like helping. Sometimes it looks like playing.
But if you keep showing up—it becomes something real.

We don't always begin with a bang.
Sometimes, we begin when we stop trying to "start right"...
and just start.

So if you're in that messy phase where things don't make perfect sense
yet—
keep doing what feels natural.
Keep fixing. Keep helping. Keep creating.

Before you know it,
you'll look up and realize—
You're already building.

XIV

Life Between the Lines on a Marksheet

There's a strange pressure that exists only in Indian households when the report card arrives.

The silence after your marks are announced is louder than any scolding. It's the kind of silence where your parents don't say they're disappointed, because they think you already know.

I lived in that silence for years.

I was never the one with glowing percentages.

Never the reason for family group celebrations.

Never the kid who got to sit in the front row on annual day.

I was the "okay" student.

Sometimes above average. Sometimes average.

Always trying to meet the cut-off for being taken seriously.

And that's where I got stuck.

In the space between the lines.

The marksheet didn't say I was trying.

It didn't say I was building websites at 13.

Didn't say I was exploring design, fiddling with code, editing pictures, writing scripts.

Didn't say I stayed up learning things no one taught.

All it said was:

Science – 47

Maths – 64

English – 81
    And that was all anyone saw.
    So I believed it.
    I started letting the marks define what I could or couldn't do.
    "I'm not good at this."
"Maybe I'm not smart enough."
"Maybe I should just pick something safe."
    That's how I landed in science.
Not out of passion. Out of pressure.
Because it looked good. Because it sounded respectable.
Because somewhere, I was trying to buy back approval.
    But science drained me.
It felt like I was wearing someone else's shoes and trying to run.
    I struggled.
Shifted streams.
Moved to commerce.
Tried CS. Failed there too.
    Every time I changed directions, I felt like I had to explain myself.
Like I owed people a justification for not being the kid they thought I would
be.
    But deep down, I wasn't lost.
I was searching.
    I wasn't confused.
I was curious.
    I didn't lack intelligence.
I lacked permission to trust my own instincts.
    The education system rewards what it can measure.
It doesn't reward curiosity.
It doesn't grade late-night learning.
It doesn't care how many side projects you start and scrap.
    And that's okay.
    Because real growth?
It rarely fits into boxes.
    The person I am today wasn't born from my academic wins.
It came from the decisions I made when I felt behind.
    From the night I cried quietly after yet another failure.
From the day I went to college just to say I showed up.
From the moment I applied for a job just to feel like I was moving.

Every small act, every shift, every fall—it taught me more than any textbook ever did.

So if your marksheet doesn't reflect your worth,

if your stream doesn't match your spirit,

if you're not where your classmates are—

Don't panic.

Because you are not your grade.

You are not your stream.

You are not the comments made on PTM day.

You are what you choose to build from here.

And if no one has told you yet—

You're doing just fine.

XV

You Don't Need a Title to Lead, Just Proof That You've Grown

We chase titles like they'll unlock doors.
But the truth is—people follow proof, not position.
There was a time when I felt underqualified.
I didn't have a college degree from a big-name school.
I didn't hold a "manager" badge.
I hadn't "worked at" the right companies.
So I stayed quiet in rooms where I actually had the most insight.
Not because I didn't know the answers—
but because I didn't feel I had the right to speak yet.
Turns out, that was never the real metric.
Over time, I realized something powerful:
People don't care what's written on your LinkedIn.
They care about what happens when they work with you.
Do you show up?
Do you deliver?
Do you make things better, clearer, smoother, smarter?
That's the real resume.
And as I kept building, helping, solving—
the "title" thing disappeared.

Clients stopped asking for my qualifications.
They started referring me to others.
Team members listened not because I demanded respect—
but because I earned it in the trenches.
I started seeing myself differently too.
Not as a freelancer.
Not as an agency.
Not even as a founder.
Just as a leader.
Not leading people, necessarily.
But leading process.
Results.
Momentum.
And that shift changed how I handled problems, pitched ideas, and made decisions.
I wasn't asking, "Am I allowed to do this?"
I was asking, "What's the best way to get this done?"
What this taught me:
Leadership is not granted.
It's revealed—through your clarity, consistency, and care.
You don't need a title to lead.
You need behavior that people want to trust.
And when you live that enough times...
the world will call you a leader—even if you never called yourself one.

XVI
Build, Break, Repeat

I've started more things than I've finished.

That's not a confession. It's a pattern.

A real one.

One that took me years to stop feeling ashamed about.

Because back then, I didn't know what I was doing.

But I couldn't sit still either.

There was Invitro.

A digital project I built with heart—clean branding, structured pitch, a proper domain.

Did it take off? No.

Because I built it with energy, but no funnel. No team. No trademark. No revenue strategy.

Then came Healthlease.

Followed by InteriorsOnEMI.

Then Fachelors—a name that made me laugh every time I said it.

Each of these had decks. Logos. Page layouts.

Some even had Instagram accounts and pitch calls.

But none of them made real money.

None of them were protected.

None of them were rooted in law, or IP, or market validation.

I didn't know the difference between copyright and trademark back then.

Didn't know that owning an idea isn't the same as protecting it.

And when people started launching similar things, I didn't fight.

Because it didn't feel like mine anymore.

So I quietly stepped back.

That's what this chapter is about.

Not the launches.

But the quiet exits.

The way I used to build something for weeks...

then lose belief in it overnight.

Delete the folder. Archive the page. Ghost the domain.

I used to think that made me a failure.

Now I know better.

It made me a builder without guidance.

When I first started offering digital services, I went wide.

SEO, SMM, ORM, content creation—you name it, I listed it.

It looked great on my profile.

Sounded smart in my proposals.

But you know what it didn't do?

Convert.

Because I didn't actually enjoy doing all of it.

And I wasn't getting clients for most of it anyway.

So I pivoted.

I stopped offering what looked good.

Started offering what got results—for both me and the client.

Designing creatives.

Writing ad copies.

Campaign briefing.

Website structuring.

These were things I could do fast, well, and without burning out.

And slowly, my self-image stopped depending on how many services I offered...

and started depending on how many I could deliver with confidence.

That was the real evolution.

Not from failure to success.

But from reactive creation to intentional building.

There's a difference between being multi-talented and being misaligned.

Back then, I was mistaking restlessness for ambition.

Now, I know:

You don't have to keep reinventing yourself to feel worthy.

You just have to find what sticks—and stick with it.

But I don't regret those broken starts.

Because every abandoned idea taught me something.

Every half-built project gave me clarity.

Every "maybe this is the one" added a layer to my instinct.

I had to go through the cycle of build, break, repeat—
to learn how to build with roots next time.

If you're in that phase right now—chasing ten ideas, burning out before you can even launch, starting fresh every month because nothing feels right...

You're not lost.

You're learning your own taste.

You're collecting your toolkit.

You're learning what not to do again.

And one day, that'll make all the difference.

Because while others wait to perfect one idea before starting...

You'll already have ten versions behind you.

And the eleventh?

That'll feel like home.

XVII

The Client Who Made Me Rebuild Myself

I never thought I'd get to sit across the table from someone who once built dreams I only saw on television.

I was just a kid when I first visited Kingdom of Dreams in Gurgaon—lights, shows, celebrities, the kind of place that made you feel like a different life existed just a few feet away from yours. So when I landed a meeting with the man who created it, years later, for work—I didn't feel nervous.

I felt small.

Not in a bad way.

But in the kind of way where your younger self suddenly shows up inside you and whispers:

"Can you believe this?"

He wasn't running Kingdom of Dreams anymore.

COVID had ruined a lot.

The business had shrunk.

He was starting over—building an adventure park in Rishikesh called Thrill Factory.

But even starting over, he was bigger than anything I'd worked on before.

I had built dozens of ecommerce sites, branding for small startups, solo entrepreneurs, and retail clients.

This was different.

This was... everything.

He didn't need a website.

He needed the whole machine:

PR. Branding. Theatre film production. Bulk WhatsApp systems. Campaign ideation. Launch strategy. Social proof. Content pipelines.

It was the first time someone trusted me with the entire marketing wheel.

And I wasn't sure I had what it took to turn it.

I showed up every week.

With a small team.

With my car.

With my own fuel.

Trying to piece together what bigger agencies were doing with teams of 20.

I tried outsourcing.

I tried scaling.

I tried saying yes to everything—even when I had no business saying yes.

Not because I wanted to impress him.

Because I didn't want to miss the moment.

I believed—if I could just deliver this, everything would change.

But the more I said yes, the more I stretched.

And eventually, I cracked.

He once asked me in a meeting, very casually,

"How much did you score in 10th?"

I told him.

Then he asked about 12th.

I told him that too.

And he looked me in the eye and said,

"That's why you're not able to do it."

It wasn't rude.

Just... real.

At least from where he stood.

But from where I sat, it stung in a way I wasn't prepared for.

Not because he was wrong.

But because part of me believed it might be true.

And in that moment, I felt like everything I had built up until now—every late night, every pitch, every deck, every idea—was reduced to my old report cards.

I kept showing up.

Kept working.

Did what I could.
But eventually, the project faded.
He never paid me.
And I never chased it.
He was running in losses. I saw that.
The place was big, but the energy felt like survival.
Still—something inside me wished he had paid.
Not just for the work, but for what it cost me to believe I could do it.
But I let it go.
Not because I wasn't angry.
But because I knew this project wasn't just a client story.
It was a mirror.
After that, I didn't crash.
I enrolled.
I applied for an Executive Program in Branding & Advertising at IIM Indore.
Not to impress anyone.
Not to prove him wrong.
But to never feel that small again.
That chapter pushed me into discomfort.
It exposed every gap I had hidden behind speed and multitasking.
And while he may never know what he triggered—
He made me rebuild how I see myself.
Not just as a doer.
But as a builder who's worth the room he walks into.
You don't always need kind mentors.
Sometimes, you need the ones who shake you without even knowing it.
And you leave—not with a cheque.
But with a fire you didn't have before.

XVIII

Self-Sabotage in Smart Clothes

For the longest time, I thought self-sabotage looked like chaos.

Missed deadlines. Poor communication. Burnout.

The loud stuff.

But what I learned is this:

Sometimes, self-sabotage looks like productivity.

It looks like working late on things that don't matter.

Redesigning a deck that was already good enough.

Spending hours planning something you're too scared to start.

It wears clean clothes. It answers emails. It attends Zoom meetings.

And yet—it quietly keeps you from going where you actually want to go.

That's the version I met in myself.

I used to tell people I was "working on something."

And I was.

Sort of.

I was tweaking, polishing, adjusting, preparing—on repeat.

I had dozens of half-ready portfolios.

Ideas for content calendars that never got published.

Clients I never followed up with because I convinced myself they probably weren't interested anymore.

All under the name of professionalism.

But what I was really doing?

Delaying exposure.

Because if I never shipped the idea,
no one could reject it.
If I never launched the site,
no one could bounce from it.
If I never posted the reel,
no one could scroll past it.

So I stayed safe—in motion, but not in momentum.

The irony is, from the outside, I looked productive.

I was always "doing."
Always busy.
Always appearing to move forward.

But deep down, I was hiding.

From criticism. From imperfection. From being found out.

"What if I go all in and still fail?"
"What if they don't like what I make?"
"What if I'm not as good as I've made them believe?"

These thoughts didn't paralyze me.
They disguised themselves as strategy.

And that made them even more dangerous.

I had to unlearn that pattern.
And it didn't happen because of a quote or a pep talk.
It happened when I got tired of watching myself play small in the name of "preparation."

So I stopped hiding behind busy.

And I started building something structured.

I went back to school.

Applied for an executive education program in Branding & Advertising at IIM Indore.
Weekend classes.
Assignments.
Case studies.
Projects that pushed me out of my comfort zone.

And alongside that—I began building what I never had before:
A real team.
Not just a marketing agency.
But a framework to put my lessons into practice—live, while learning.

Designers.
Editors.

Writers.
Campaign managers.
Production team.
Talent acquisition.
Account coordinators.
The first six months were trial by fire.
Interviews. Team changes. Conflicts.
People came in. Some left. Some stayed.
Everyone taught me something.
And while I was building that team,
I was building a new version of me.
One that could balance study and structure.
One that wasn't performing anymore—but leading.
I'd learn something in class on Saturday,
and apply it to a client project on Monday.
No waiting. No fluff. No fear.
This wasn't about proving anyone wrong.
Not the clients. Not the people who doubted me.
Not even the man who once tied my potential to my high school scores.
This was for me.
To stop editing my ambition to match my fear.
To stop pausing just because I wasn't ready.
To finally start acting like the builder I knew I could become.
So if you're stuck in overthinking...
If you're working, but nothing's moving...
If you've got more drafts than launches...
Step back.
Check your reflection.
Ask if your 'busy' is actually a disguise.
Then build it anyway.
Even scared.
Even small.
Even slow.
Because the only way out of self-sabotage—
is self-leadership.

XIX

The Success I Wasn't Ready For

Success doesn't always feel like a win.

Sometimes, it feels like overwhelm.

Like suddenly getting what you prayed for—then freezing because you don't know what to do with it.

That's what happened to me.

Not all at once.

But slowly, subtly, silently—success crept in through the cracks.

Clients started coming in.

Real ones. Not favours. Not friends.

People who didn't know me, but trusted me.

Budgets got bigger. So did expectations.

What used to be a side hustle was now a company.

What used to be a pitch deck was now a retained account.

And what used to be a solo operation with a Canva Pro account and sleepless hustle...

suddenly had invoices, calendars, teammates, targets.

This was what I wanted.

This was what I'd worked for.

And yet—

I didn't feel ready.

I wasn't prepared for the pressure of being relied on.

Wasn't prepared for the version of leadership that required me to be stable, consistent, present—even when I didn't feel like it.

I had spent so long learning how to start things…
I didn't know how to hold them.

I didn't know how to sustain the weight of what I built.

There were weeks I'd lie awake wondering:

"Can I actually handle this?"
"Am I just faking it well enough for people not to notice?"
"What if it all falls apart tomorrow?"

I stopped celebrating wins because they scared me.
Because now that people were watching, the fall would feel harder.

I didn't realize how much I was tied to being the underdog.
How safe it felt to be "on the way up."
Because once you're in the room, the story changes.

You have to speak up.
You have to own your voice.
You have to deliver—not for praise, but for proof.

One of the hardest things I had to learn during that time was this:
Success won't save you from insecurity.
It'll just meet it at a higher level.

All the old self-doubt I thought I'd left behind—
It came back, dressed in new clothes.

Now it didn't say, "You're not good enough."
Now it said, "You can't afford to mess this up."

But in the middle of all that overwhelm…
I also grew.

Not by doing more.
But by learning how to breathe inside the pressure.

I stopped trying to do everything alone.
Started hiring smarter. Delegating better.
I created systems. SOPs. Processes I used to mock when I was hustling solo.

And most importantly—
I started treating myself like a CEO, not a freelancer with ambition.

That shift didn't make the success feel less scary.
But it gave me a container to hold it.

And that changed everything.

So if you're in a season where everything you wanted is finally showing
up—
and you're secretly terrified?

You're not failing.

You're stretching.

You're becoming the version of you who can actually carry the weight of what you once only dreamed about.

And that takes time.

That takes presence.

That takes belief—especially on the days it doesn't come naturally.

Success doesn't always feel like a celebration.

Sometimes, it feels like surrender.

To responsibility. To pressure. To your own growth.

But if you can sit in that discomfort,

and still keep going?

You're already succeeding in ways no metric can ever measure.

XX

When You're the Product

There comes a point in your journey where you realize—
You're not just selling your service.
You're selling yourself.
Not in the loud, influencer way.
But in the deeply vulnerable way where your name, your energy, your mindset—
become the brand.
And that hit me harder than I expected.
Because up until then, I was safe behind the work.
Behind the logo.
Behind the decks.
Behind the Canva files and Google Docs and endless revisions.
People hired "Pitchers Global."
People paid for content, campaigns, websites.
But one day, a client said it out loud:
"We're not hiring you for the deliverables. We're hiring you because of how you think."
And that shifted everything.
Suddenly, the pressure changed.
Now, my clarity mattered more than my checklist.
My leadership was worth more than my layout.
My energy decided the room—not the brief.

And while part of me felt honored...
another part of me felt exposed.

Because when you are the product, there's nowhere to hide.

You can't say "I'm just the designer."
You can't say "I'm just doing my part."
You are the part.

If you're confused, the project's confused.
If you're inconsistent, the output is shaky.
If your belief is low, the team's momentum dips.

It's personal now.

This wasn't just about building a brand anymore.
It was about becoming one.

Which meant:

Showing up even when I didn't feel "on."

Making decisions that aligned with who I was, not just what looked good.

Saying no to clients who were technically profitable—but emotionally expensive.

Sharing stories from my life, not just my portfolio.

Standing for something more than services.

And trust me, that wasn't easy.

Because becoming the brand meant reintroducing myself constantly.

"Who are you really?"
"What do you stand for?"
"What do you want people to feel when they interact with your work?"

Questions I avoided for years suddenly became non-negotiable.

It also meant I had to face parts of myself I'd buried under tasks.

Like the need to be liked.
The fear of being misunderstood.
The habit of hiding behind perfection.

But the more I brought me into the work,
the more the work started attracting the right people.

Clients didn't just want delivery.
They wanted decisions.
They wanted insight.
They wanted alignment.

And for the first time, I stopped trying to "scale."
And started trying to resonate.

When you're the product, you don't get the luxury of detachment.

But you do get the freedom of authenticity.
Your story sells.
Your scars sell.
Your lens, your rhythm, your gut instinct—those become assets.
And the best part?
You don't have to compete.
Because no one else can copy you when you're being you.
So if you've been wondering when to step up as the face,
when to stop hiding behind the logo,
when to let people see the builder behind the brand—
Here's your sign:
You already are the product.
Now it's time to own it.

XXI
Reinventing Yourself Every Quarter

I used to think reinvention was dramatic.

New city. New role. Shaved head.

A big announcement. A grand reveal.

Some visible reset to prove you've changed.

But I learned something quieter.

Reinvention can happen in the form of a sentence you stop saying.

An offer you quietly remove from your service list.

An instinct you finally start listening to.

It happens in private long before it shows up in public.

Every few months, I'd feel it—a restlessness.

Not burnout. Not boredom.

Just a nudge in the back of my mind saying,

"This version of you has done its job.

It's time for an update."

At first, I ignored it.

Tried to stay consistent.

Kept running the same funnels, using the same templates, serving the same types of clients.

But the work felt heavy.

My calendar felt misaligned.

I didn't want to take calls anymore, not because I was tired—

but because something in me was shifting.

And if I didn't shift with it, I knew I'd resent the very thing I once loved.

So I began embracing reinvention.

Not as a collapse. But as a rhythm.

Every quarter, I asked myself:

What feels heavy?

What am I saying yes to that drains me?

What do I keep postponing because I don't actually believe in it anymore?

And most importantly:

What would I do differently if no one was watching?

That last question changed everything.

One quarter, I dropped three services that made me money—but no longer made me proud.

Another quarter, I stopped chasing agency-sized clients and focused on founders who resonated with my pace and purpose.

Sometimes, I changed how I introduced myself.

Sometimes, I changed my schedule.

Sometimes, I changed my pricing.

Not to confuse my audience.

But to stay honest with myself.

And you know what happened?

I stopped feeling stuck in my own growth.

Because I no longer owed anyone the same version of me forever.

Here's the truth they don't put in motivational quotes:

You don't need a rock bottom to reinvent.

Sometimes you just need an honest check-in.

And reinvention isn't about becoming someone new.

It's about becoming more of who you already are—

minus the noise, the pressure, and the outdated playbooks.

So if you're feeling it—the itch to shift, the guilt for outgrowing your own strategy, the hesitation to let go of what once worked...

Let this be your permission:

You're allowed to evolve.

Not just annually.

Not just after a burnout.

Every season. Every cycle. Every quarter.

Not because you're inconsistent.

But because you're alive.

XXII

Money, Doubt & the Days You Still Show Up

Let's talk about the days when you're not building out of inspiration—
you're building because the rent is due.

When "purpose" takes a back seat to "payment received."
When you still show up... not with pride, but with pressure.

I've lived more of those days than I've shared.
And I don't think enough people admit it.

There were weeks I'd finish client work, deliver everything on time, and still feel like I was failing—because my bank account didn't match my energy.

There were mornings I'd wake up to emails that said,

"We're going in another direction,"
while the only direction I wanted was forward.

Some nights, I'd stare at the screen, refreshing the invoice tracker, re-reading follow-ups I never got a reply to.
Not because I was desperate—
But because I was quietly afraid:

"Is this even sustainable?"

Money isn't just numbers when you're self-made.
It's proof. It's safety.
It's how you measure value in a world that forgets to say "thank you."

But here's what I learned—
Money and self-worth can't sit in the same account.

Because when they do, one dip in revenue makes you question your relevance.

One slow month feels like a personal failure.

One unpaid project makes you wonder if you're really cut out for this.

That's the slippery slope I had to climb out of.

I had to start separating the numbers from the narrative.

I had to remind myself that showing up with doubt doesn't mean I'm weak.

It means I'm human.

It means I care.

It means I'm building not just a business—but resilience.

Because not every season is harvest.

Some seasons are holding on.

Some seasons are repeating yourself until someone listens.

Some seasons are doing your best work with zero applause.

And in those seasons, I found something more valuable than profit:

Pace.

Pace is what kept me moving when motivation disappeared.

Pace is what made me work even when I didn't feel inspired.

Pace is what helped me rebuild after a failed month—without needing to rebrand or run.

Not because I was superhuman.

But because I'd decided:

If I could still show up on my worst day,

I could build something unshakable.

So yes, money matters.

Doubt is real.

And some days will feel like you're giving more than you're getting.

But if you're still showing up?

You've already won more than most people ever will.

Because consistency under pressure is a form of leadership no one claps for.

But one day, it'll be the reason they believe in you.

XXIII

The Hidden Gift of Not Having a Team

We're all sold the same story: grow your team, build an empire, scale fast.
But what if your breakthrough doesn't come from adding people—
It comes from removing pressure?

There was a time I had over 25 people working under me.
15 in-house. 10 remote.
Writers, editors, designers, campaign managers.

And while we got a lot done,
we also dropped a lot.
Delays, miscommunications, dependency loops.
There was always someone waiting on someone else.

It felt big.
But it didn't feel light.

Fast forward to now?

I've got a core team of four.
And the rest of my extended "team" is made up of 21 AI tools—smart, fast,
trained to work like my second brain.

What once took me 8 hours with 3 people,
now takes 30 minutes—solo.

Writing. Editing. Ideation. Planning. Voiceover. Design drafts.
All streamlined.

Because I didn't build a big agency.
I built an efficient engine.

Here's the part no one tells you:
You don't need more people.
You need better systems.
And right now, the smartest system you can build...
is learning how to use AI like it's part of your creative brain.
Not to cheat.
But to speed up the boring parts so you can focus on the bold ones.
I don't feel outdated.
I feel upgraded.
Because while most people fear being replaced by AI,
I've replaced most of the overwhelm with AI.
I stopped saying:
"I need someone to do this for me."
And started asking:
"How can I do this faster, better, smarter—with tools?"
And that one shift?
It gave me time, freedom, and most importantly—flow.
What this taught me:
Your business doesn't need to look big to feel powerful.
It needs to move smart.
It needs to run light.
And it needs to feel sustainable—for you.
You can choose to build a company with 50 people.
Or build a company with 5 people and 50 well-trained tools.
Because in the world we're heading into...
AI won't replace humans.
But humans who use AI will replace the ones who don't.

XXIV
The 3 A.M. Business Plan

Some of my best ideas didn't come during client calls.
They came at 3 a.m.—
when the world was asleep,
and I was still wide awake, not by choice,
but because my mind wouldn't shut up.
    I used to hate those nights.
    Lying on the mattress, eyes burning, tabs open on the laptop,
overthinking everything from deliverables to dreams.
Trying to remember if I replied to that client.
Replaying a line from a meeting I wish I'd worded better.
Googling things like
    "how to build a scalable business"
while also wondering how to scale my energy without breaking down.
    I never called it a "business plan" back then.
    It was a brain dump.
A loose Notion doc.
Scattered WhatsApp notes to myself.
Screenshots. Spreadsheets with more ideas than income.
Mind maps that started in clarity and ended in chaos.
    But somewhere in that chaos—
things started making sense.
    Not all at once.
But enough to keep going.
    I didn't have a co-founder.
No investor. No mentor sitting with me at coffee shops giving me wisdom

bombs.

Just me.

And the business I was building wasn't just for revenue.

It was for relevance.

To feel like I mattered.

To feel like what I was creating had weight.

To feel like I wasn't wasting my life chasing approval disguised as success.

Those late nights gave me that space.

Because in the dark, there was no one to impress.

No strategy to sell.

Just brutal honesty.

And quiet ambition.

The 3 a.m. business plan isn't about structure.

It's about surrender.

It's when you finally ask yourself things like:

"What am I really trying to build?"

"What if this all works—can I actually handle it?"

"What would I build if I wasn't trying to prove anything?"

That's when real answers show up.

Not always practical.

But always personal.

I wrote half of this book in those hours.

Rebuilt services. Rethought offers.

I created team structures, launch plans, content ideas—

not when I was most focused,

but when I was most honest.

And that's what I've realized over time:

Your business doesn't just need vision.

It needs vulnerability.

Not the kind you post on social media.

The kind you admit to yourself when no one's watching.

The kind that says—

"I'm scared.

I want this badly.

I don't have it all figured out.

But I'm not quitting."

So if you're up late, unsure, scribbling half-baked ideas into your phone...

If your plans live in voice notes and recycled Trello boards...

Don't discard them.

That might be the beginning of something powerful.
Not perfect.
But true.

Because some of the most valuable companies in the world...
started in rooms with no light, no funding, no noise.

Just someone with a restless mind
and the courage to build anyway.

XXV
Journaling to Meet Myself Again

I didn't start journaling to heal.
I started because I had no one to talk to who would understand the mess in my mind.

Friends could give advice.
Family could offer concern.
But some thoughts didn't need solutions.
They just needed space.

So I wrote.
Some days it was a few lines.
Other days, it poured like confession.

Most of it wasn't structured.
It wasn't bullet journaling or morning pages or productivity tracking.

It was survival.
I wrote when I didn't trust myself.
Wrote when I couldn't remember why I was doing all this.
Wrote when clients didn't pay, when ideas didn't land, when confidence vanished without notice.

Sometimes I'd write things I didn't believe yet—
as if saying them would make them real.

"I'll get through this phase."
"This campaign will lead to something bigger."
"I'm not stuck. Just stretching."

And weirdly, it helped.

Not instantly.

But gradually.

Because journaling didn't solve my problems.

It helped me stay close to them—without being consumed.

That's when I realized:

Journaling is not for answers.

It's for awareness.

It gave me patterns.

I could look back and see what triggered burnout.

What gave me energy.

Which days I lied to myself and which days I told the truth.

I noticed how my biggest dips often came after weeks of pretending everything was fine.

How I got most creative when I had nothing to prove.

How much of my anxiety came from hiding.

And no, this wasn't therapy.

But it was a form of self-trust.

Because when you document your journey—

you stop gaslighting yourself later.

You can't pretend the phase wasn't hard when you've written pages about it.

You can't forget your small wins when you've inked them down at midnight.

Journaling gave me evidence that I was evolving—even when life looked still.

Eventually, it became a habit.

Not a daily ritual. Not a productivity hack.

Just... a checkpoint.

A way to say:

"Hey. How are you doing—not as the founder, not as the team leader, not as the doer—but as a human?"

And the answers I wrote were sometimes sharp.

Sometimes poetic.

Often, uncomfortable.

But always honest.

You don't need a fancy notebook.

You don't need prompts.

You don't need a reason.

You just need a moment of pause—
and the willingness to face what comes up when you finally stop pretending
you're fine.
Because in a world that moves fast,
writing is how I slowed down enough to meet myself again.
And every time I did,
I remembered:
I wasn't lost.
I was just buried under noise.

XXVI

The Phone Isn't the Problem

The Phone Isn't the Problem
There was a time I blamed my phone for everything:
The lack of focus.
The slow workdays.
The anxiety.
The constant need to check, scroll, refresh, reply.
I called it a "distraction machine."
Said I'd go on digital detoxes.
Put up Instagram stories like:
"Taking a break. Need some offline peace."
Only to come back two days later, no less distracted, just slightly more guilty.
Until one day, I stopped blaming the phone.
And started asking what I was actually running from.
The phone wasn't the problem.
My relationship with attention was.
Because when I was focused, it didn't matter what notifications popped up.
And when I wasn't...
even airplane mode couldn't save me from my own mind.
I didn't need to quit the screen.
I needed to question what I was using it to avoid.

Most of the time?

It was silence.

Silence scared me.

Because silence meant I had to hear myself.

And some days, the inner dialogue wasn't kind.

So I'd pick up the phone.

To escape.

To avoid.

To fill the gap between "I'm not doing enough" and "I don't know what to do next."

Endless reels. Endless tabs.

A new productivity tool. A new marketing hack. A new creator to compare myself to.

And by the end of it, I didn't feel inspired.

I felt... defeated.

So I tried something different.

Not a detox.

A redesign.

I stopped making my phone the enemy.

I made it accountable to my actual life.

I turned off every single notification except messages from key people.

I deleted apps I was using more for habit than for help.

I rearranged my home screen based on energy, not entertainment.

And most importantly, I started asking:

"When I pick up my phone, what am I trying to feel?"

Sometimes the answer was productivity.

Other times, it was connection.

But often—it was escape.

And that's when I learned:

The phone isn't the villain.

It just reveals what you're running from.

Now, my phone is a tool.

Not a therapy session.

Not a dopamine drip.

Not a distraction I pretend I can't control.

It holds my work, my notes, my screenshots, my ideas.

It helps me build.

But it no longer breaks my rhythm.

And that took time.
Because breaking patterns is harder than breaking apps.
So if your phone's been stealing your focus...
If you keep deleting Instagram only to reinstall it three hours later...
If you've convinced yourself that the only way to work is to disappear from the internet entirely...
Pause.
Don't punish yourself.
Ask yourself.
Restructure with grace.
Because you don't need to escape your phone.
You just need to reclaim your intention.

XXVII

Discipline: The Only Cheat Code I Found

I've tried everything.

Productivity apps.

Pomodoro timers.

Noise-cancelling headphones.

Vision boards.

Motivational quotes pasted on my wall.

Tried working with music. Without music. With a team. Without one.

Tried planning the week. Planning the day. Not planning at all.

And after everything I've tested, downloaded, scheduled, and abandoned...

Only one thing stayed.

Discipline.

Uncool. Unsexy.

Not a trending hashtag.

But the only thing that kept me from falling apart on the days my mood did.

Discipline didn't make me perfect.

It just made me predictable—to myself.

It meant I still journaled on days I didn't feel profound.

Still sent the email when self-doubt tried to delay it.

Still showed up for the team even when I wanted to disappear.

Still opened the laptop and got to work—not because I felt like it,

but because it was time.

I used to think people with discipline were rigid.
Like they were trying to force themselves into systems and routines out of fear.
    But I learned the truth:
    Discipline isn't restriction.
It's relief.
    Because when the rest of your world is noisy,
discipline gives you something to hold on to.
    You stop negotiating with yourself.
    No more:
    "Should I do it today?"
"Do I feel ready?"
"Is this the right vibe?"
    You just do it.
And that's where momentum is born.
    In a world obsessed with hacks,
this is the cheat code no one wants to hear:
    Do the work.
Even when it's boring.
Especially when no one's watching.
And most of all—when your future self is quietly counting on you.
    There were days I didn't want to open the client dashboard.
Days when every part of me felt scattered.
Days I thought: "One skipped task won't matter."
    But I'd do it anyway.
Not because I'm better.
But because I'd lived through what happens when you stop showing up.
    Momentum dies fast.
And getting it back is 10x harder.
    So now I treat discipline like a business partner.
    It doesn't shout.
Doesn't clap.
Doesn't care if I'm in a creative mood.
    It just meets me where I am and says:
    "Let's keep building."
    And that's why we're still here.

XXVIII

Your Brand is What You Heal

I used to think branding was about how you present yourself.
The right color palette.
A catchy tagline.
A story that sounds bold, yet relatable.
But the more I built, the more I learned:
Your brand is not what you post.
It's what you've processed.
It's how you think under pressure.
How you recover from setbacks.
How you lead when no one claps.
When I first started offering services, I focused on looking legit.
Neat proposals.
Confident copy.
A polished pitch deck.
But deep inside, I hadn't healed the insecurity of being called "average" in school.
I hadn't addressed the fear of rejection.
I hadn't forgiven myself for the projects that didn't take off.
So even though my surface looked smooth,
my decisions were coming from fear.
I'd underprice.
Over-deliver.

Say yes to things I didn't want to do—just to feel worthy.

And it showed.

Not in the design.

But in the energy.

Clients might not have said it out loud…

but they could sense I didn't fully believe in myself yet.

That's when I started connecting the dots.

Every phase of healing shifted how I worked.

And every time I grew inside, my brand grew outside.

When I healed my need to be validated—

I stopped chasing low-value work.

When I healed my fear of being seen—

I started showing up in my content with more honesty.

When I healed my burnout patterns—

I built systems instead of surviving on energy.

It wasn't a strategy change.

It was a self-worth upgrade.

Your brand is not just what you create.

It's the **version of you** that does the creating.

And that version is shaped every time you choose courage over chaos.

Every time you set a boundary.

Every time you say, "I'm not available for that anymore."

If you've ever wondered why your brand doesn't feel aligned—

look inside, not just at your feed.

Ask:

What story am I trying to prove through this work?

What part of me still believes I have to "perform" to be paid?

What have I outgrown, but haven't outlived publicly yet?

Because your business will grow to the level of your inner stability.

Not your strategy.

You don't have to be healed to start.

But if you want to build something that lasts—

you'll have to keep doing the work.

Not just on your funnels.

But on yourself.

XXIX

Nobody Cares. But You Should.

This is going to sound cold.
But it might be the most liberating thing I've learned:
Nobody cares.
They don't care if you posted today.
They don't care if you stayed up all night building.
They don't care if you designed the entire funnel yourself.
They don't care if you launched something that took months of effort and got 12 likes.
And that used to hurt.
I'd upload something I was proud of—
and refresh the feed, waiting for proof that it mattered.
A comment. A share. Some sign of applause.
Sometimes it came.
Sometimes it didn't.
And the emotional rollercoaster that followed?
Exhausting.
But then I stopped waiting.
Not because I gave up—
But because I finally got it:
It's not their job to care.
It's mine.

It's my job to believe in the story before it's trending.
To show up before anyone claps.
To continue even when nobody's watching.
That's not ego.
That's ownership.
Nobody owes you recognition.
Not your friends.
Not your family.
Not the audience that watches but doesn't engage.
And once you make peace with that,
you free yourself from performing.
You stop asking,
"Is anyone noticing me?"
And start asking,
"Am I proud of this even if no one says a word?"
That shift changed how I worked.
I stopped obsessing over numbers.
Started obsessing over integrity.
Over making things I'd revisit five years later and still feel good about.
Some of the most important things I've built started in silence.
This book.
My journal entries.
The version of Pitchers Global that no one saw during the reworks.
The skill sets I practiced when no clients were asking for them.
None of it was public.
None of it went viral.
But all of it mattered.
Because the consistency that built me?
Was never for display.
If you're building something right now and wondering if it's worth it—
it is.
Even if no one cares.
Even if no one claps.
Even if the numbers look disappointing.
Because the thing you're making?
It's not just a project.
It's a promise.
To the version of you who chose not to quit.

Let them scroll.
Let them skip.
Let them not care.
You?
You show up anyway.
Because one day, they'll look back and call it impressive.
But by then,
you'll already know it was important—
because you were the first one who cared.

XXX

The Community I Wanted Didn't Exist, So I Started Building It

At some point, you stop looking for the right place to belong—
and start building it yourself.

I didn't plan to create a community.

There was no business model, no landing page, no hashtag campaign.

There was just this recurring feeling:

"Why are we all trying to figure things out alone?"

I'd meet people—brilliant, brave, burnt out—

who had ideas, ambition, even skill...

but no safe space to grow with others who get it.

No one clapped for their progress.

No one asked them what they needed.

No one reminded them that building is hard—but they weren't weird for still trying.

And I thought...

Why not create that space?

Not a platform.

Not a cult.

Just a quiet, meaningful space for people who are in-between:

Between who they were and who they want to become

Between idea and execution

Between burnout and breakthrough
That seed became Kumohana.
No grand launch.
Just honest conversations.
Shared tools.
Collaborative learning.
Real people doing real work without pretending it's perfect.
Some came in looking for skills.
Others came in looking for clarity.
Many didn't even know what they were looking for.
They just knew they didn't want to grow alone anymore.
And that was enough.
What started as a side note on my journey became a core part of it.
And without even trying to "scale" it—
Kumohana started pulling the right people in.
People who wanted to build.
People who wanted to contribute.
People who were tired of chasing... and ready to create with peace.
The thing you need most might be the thing you're meant to create.
If you feel like there's no place that fully understands your journey—
maybe you're not lost.
Maybe you're just meant to build that place yourself.
It doesn't have to be perfect.
It doesn't have to be popular.
It just has to be honest.
And if it is—people will come.
You don't have to build with everyone.
But don't build without anyone.
You'll go further.
And it'll feel less lonely.

XXXI

Dear Reader: You're Not Late. You're Just Building.

If no one's told you this lately—
Let me be the one to say it:

You're not late.

I don't care what your age is.

I don't care what everyone else on LinkedIn is doing.

I don't care if it feels like you're the last person in your circle who hasn't "made it."

Because the truth is—there's no actual timeline.

There's just pressure.

And most of it? You didn't even choose.

Some of the most incredible people I know didn't peak at 25.

They didn't "crack the code" in their 20s.

They didn't follow the rulebook.

They experimented.

Failed publicly.

Restarted quietly.

Built something small.

Let it die.

Started again.

And in the middle of all that trial and error—
They found themselves.
That's the real win.
The world will tell you there's a clock.
That by 30 you should have X.
That by 35 you should have Y.
That if you haven't scaled, exited, published, or married by now—
you're behind.
But behind what, exactly?
What metric are we using?
Because if I'm being honest—
Some of the richest people I've met are emotionally bankrupt.
And some of the slowest builders I know are building with the deepest alignment.
You get to decide what "on time" feels like.
If you've taken detours, paused your dreams, chosen healing over hustle…
You're not slow.
You're just self-aware.
If you've started late because no one handed you the playbook…
You're not unqualified.
You're building from scratch—and that's a skill most people never master.
If you're still figuring it out…
If you're unsure, overwhelmed, inconsistent, hopeful—
you're human.
And this chapter is your reminder:
You're not behind.
You're just building.
Quietly. Bravely. At your own speed.
And that's more than enough.
So breathe.
The people who are "ahead" aren't your competition.
They're just on a different chapter.
And yours?
It's being written—word by word, lesson by lesson—
on days when no one's watching but you still show up anyway.
That's progress.
That's momentum.
That's what becoming looks like.

XXXII

This Isn't a Success Story. It's a Starting Point.

If you came looking for a happily-ever-after,
this book might've disappointed you.

There's no luxury car in the driveway.
No Forbes feature.
No "I made my first crore at 25" plot twist.

Because this isn't that story.

This is a story of someone who fell behind.
Who switched paths.
Who started late.
Who doubted, drifted, reset, and rebuilt—quietly.

Someone who didn't wait to be discovered.
But decided to discover themselves.

And maybe, that's where this whole book was headed from the start.

I didn't write this because I "made it."
I wrote it because somewhere along the way,
I mentored myself out of the fog.

I stopped waiting for someone to guide me, to push me, to tell me I was doing well.
I gave that to myself.

And in doing so, I learned something:

"Clarity doesn't come with answers.
It comes when you stop running from the questions."
So if you're here at the end, wondering what to do with this—
Don't rush to act.
Don't force some big change.
Just sit with it.
Ask yourself:
What part of me have I been ignoring?
What skill have I already been sharpening without noticing?
What old version of me am I ready to finally let go of?
What if the next breakthrough doesn't come from learning more… but from trusting what I already know?
You don't need to become the next big thing.
You just need to become more of yourself, every day.
That's where the power is.
That's where the peace is.
And if you ever feel like you're slipping back into the fog—
Come back to these pages.
Not for advice.
But for reminders.
Because the truth is:
You've already started.
And now…
you know how to mentor yourself.

XXXIII

A Letter to the Builder in You

You don't need another plan right now.
You don't need another tool, another strategy, or a better tagline.
What you need— is a reminder.
That what you're building matters.
That the quiet effort counts.
That you don't have to go viral to be valid.
That slow growth is still growth.
And that you—
The you who stayed.
The you who tried again.
The you who rebuilt in silence while everyone else watched louder
people—
You're already becoming.
Even on the days it doesn't look like it.
To the builder in you:
I know it gets heavy.
The pressure to look like you've figured it out.
The need to explain yourself to people who don't get it.
The weight of your own expectations.
But I want you to know this:
It's okay to rest.
It's okay to be unsure.

It's okay to build slowly, quietly, awkwardly.
What matters isn't how polished your journey looks.
What matters is that it's yours.
And that you're choosing to keep going—
not because it's easy,
but because it's right.
For you.
You've probably outgrown things you once prayed for.
You've probably said yes to things that drained you—just to prove you
could.
You've probably had seasons where your best work went unnoticed.
That's not failure.
That's the curriculum.
And here you are now,
reading this.
Still showing up.
Still building.
Not because you have to.
But because something inside you refuses to settle.
That's rare.
That's powerful.
That's why this book was written.
Not to give you answers—
but to remind you you're not alone.
So when the next phase gets hard—
When the likes dip.
When the money slows.
When your motivation disappears again...
Come back to this:
You're not behind.
You're not invisible.
You're not done.
You're just building.
And the version of you on the other side?
They're already proud.

Epilogue: You Are The Next Chapter

If this book felt familiar,
it's because it was never just about me.
It was always about you.
Your hesitations.
Your half-finished plans.
Your ideas that don't yet have a name.
Your quiet resilience no one sees.
This wasn't a story wrapped in a bow.
It was a mirror—
with fingerprints, smudges, and real reflections.
If you're still figuring it out...
you're not behind.
You're building.
And you don't need perfect clarity to keep moving forward.
You just need to keep showing up—
with intention,
with grace,
and with trust.
You've got this.
And if you forget,
come back.
These words aren't going anywhere.

Build Your Version, Your Way

This section isn't a blueprint.

It's a mirror.

Use it however you need.

No pressure. Just prompts.

1. What season are you in right now?

❑ Building

❑ Rebuilding

❑ Breaking quietly

❑ Starting over

❑ Resting

❑ Don't know yet (and that's okay)

2. What do you need to let go of to move forward?

(Write it. Burn it. Archive it. Release it.)

3. What's one story you've been telling yourself that no longer serves you?

Rewrite it in one sentence.

4. Name one thing you've built that no one saw—but you're still proud of.

Let it count.

5. Define "success" in your own words—not borrowed ones.

Then ask yourself: Am I living toward that?

6. What does your next quiet move look like?

(Not the loud, public one. The real one.)

This is where your pages begin.

This isn't just a book.

It's a tool.

A trigger.

A turning point.

Below are 3 powerful exercises to help you move from awareness to action. Do them honestly. No filters. No performance.

Exercise 1: The 100-Truth List

The secret clarity blueprint you never learned in school.

Write 100 statements that start with:

"I believe..."

"I fear..."

"I need..."

"I regret..."

"I want..."

"I love..."

This will exhaust you. It will also reveal you. Somewhere between line 43 and 71, you'll write something that breaks you open. That's your starting line.

Exercise 2: The 24-Hour Visibility Challenge Do something uncomfortable that makes you visible. Today.

Go live. Share a journal entry. Send a voice note to someone who inspires you.

No prep. No perfection. Just realness.

This single act of being seen will shift your self-respect more than reading 100 books.

Exercise 3: The "No More" List

Your silent detox. Write this somewhere you can see daily.

List 10 things you're no longer available for. Not just habits—but patterns.

Example:

No more replying just to be liked.

No more overworking to prove I'm capable.

No more staying small so others feel big.

Read it daily. Act like it's law.

Journaling Prompts to Revisit Anytime:

What am I truly tired of pretending?

Where in my life am I performing instead of participating?

What do I need to forgive myself for?

What's one truth I've been avoiding?

Who would I become if I stopped trying to be impressive?

Reminder: You're not reading this because you're behind.
You're here because you're ready.
Go build the version of you that no longer needs to explain itself.

Bonus Exercise:

Write a letter from your future self to your present self.
Start it with:
"Hey, I know things feel unclear sometimes, but here's what I want you to remember..."
Read it back in 30 days.
I'll be rooting for you—quietly, always.

Author's Note: Why I Wrote This

I didn't write this to prove anything.
I wrote it because I never had this book when I needed it.
I had to stitch together my own path—between survival and
self-discovery, between doubt and design, between the fear of starting over
and the joy of figuring things out for real.
This book is that path.
And if it helps even one person find clarity or breathe easier... it was worth
it.
No part of your journey is wasted.
Every pause, detour, breakdown—it's all data.
And eventually, it all turns into direction.
Thank you for reading my notes while I figured things out.
Now it's your turn to write yours.
– Ayush Garg

www.ingramcontent.com/pod-product-compliance
Lightning Source LLC
Chambersburg PA
CBHW062235150726
47991CB00006B/2585